HUMILIATION AND INSULT

IT RESULTED INTO MAHABHARAT WAR

AF559356

KRISHNA MURARI SONI

Copyright © Krishna Murari Soni
All Rights Reserved.

This book has been published with all efforts taken to make the material error-free after the consent of the author. However, the author and the publisher do not assume and hereby disclaim any liability to any party for any loss, damage, or disruption caused by errors or omissions, whether such errors or omissions result from negligence, accident, or any other cause.

While every effort has been made to avoid any mistake or omission, this publication is being sold on the condition and understanding that neither the author nor the publishers or printers would be liable in any manner to any person by reason of any mistake or omission in this publication or for any action taken or omitted to be taken or advice rendered or accepted on the basis of this work. For any defect in printing or binding the publishers will be liable only to replace the defective copy by another copy of this work then available.

Contents

Contents

Preface

The Mahabharat war was fought in Kurukshetra, a place in Haryana state of India, thus also known as Kurukshetra war. Since, almost all the kings of Bharat (old name of India) participated in Kurukshetra war, it is called as Mahabharat war.

The war was led by two family factions known as Kauravas and Pandavas but their supporters also joined it. It is said that the war was fought for the throne of Hastinapur, a place in district Meerut of present Uttar Pradesh of India though it appears that it was not for the throne but to take revenge, mostly revenge of the humiliation and insult by some individuals, princes, kings, and princesses of that period.

A mega war does not last long as destruction in such a war becomes huge, both in terms of resources and lives so also Mahabharat war lasted only for eighteen days in which all the warriors from Kauravas' side and most of them from Pandavas' side were killed including all the sons of Pandavas.

In entire Mahabharat war, it was only Lord Krishna who participated into the battle without any weapon though he was a great warrior but made huge difference to Pandavas as Arjun chose him over his powerful army. Duryodhana chose his army and lost the war. It proved that even a great unarmed leader is more powerful than thousands of soldiers.

In this book, few incidences are described which gives a clear message that we should not humiliate or insult anyone whether poor, rich, powerful, powerless, man, woman, friend, enemy, relative or a common man as it leads to destruction.

(Krishna Murari Soni)

CHAPTER ONE

About the Characters

1. Abhimanyu was the son of Arjun and Subhadra.
2. Amba, Ambe and Ambalika were princesses of Kashi king.
3. Arjun was third Pandav, son of Kunti, a great archer and close friend of Krishna, married to Draupadi and Subhadra.
4. Ashwatthama was the son of Guru Dronacharya.
5. Ashwanis or Ashwani Kumars were the deities of medicines and health and sons of Surya.
6. Balram was elder brother of Krishna.
7. Bhima was second Pandav, elder being Yudhishthir. Arjun was younger to Bhima.
8. Bhishma whose name was Devavrat was the son of king Shantanu of Hastinapur and Ganga and grandfather of both Pandavas and Kauravas, who called him Pitamah.
9. Bhurishrawa was grandson of king Bahalika, brother of Shantanu.
10. Brahaspati was the Guru of deities.
11. Chekitan was the son of king Dhristketu and king of Kaikaya.
12. Chitrangad and Vichitravirya were the sons of king Shantanu and Satyavati.

13. Chyavana was a sage.
14. Dharamraj was the deity of *dharma* and death.
15. Dhristketu was the king of Chedi and army general of Pandavas' army in Mahabharat war.
16. Dhritrashtra was the elder son of Vichitravirya, king of Hastinapur. He was blind by birth, due to which his younger brother Pandu was made the king of Hastinapur however after immature death of Pandu, he became the king of Hastinapur.
17. Draupadi was wife of daughter of Drupad, married to Pandavas.
18. Dronacharya was the guru (teacher) of Pandavas and Kauravas. He was the childhood friend of king Drupad who insulted him after becoming the king. He had one son by named Ashwatthama.
19. Drupad was the king of Panchal. Dhristdumn, Draupadi and Shikhandi (born as girl Shikhandini) were his children.
20. Dushashan was younger brother of Duryodhana.
21. Durvasa was a great sage, also known for his anger if someone did not follow his directions or respected him.
22. Duryodhana was the eldest son of Dhritrashtra and his wife Gandhari. Dhritrashtra and Gandhari had one hundred sons and a daughter named Dushala who was married to Jaydrath.
23. Gandeev was the name of the bow of Arjun.
24. Ganga is the name of holy river in India and worshipped in human form also.
25. Ghatotkach was son of Bhima and Hidimba.
26. Hastinapur is a place near Meerut city in Uttar Pradesh state of India.
27. Hidimba was the wife of Bhima.
28. Indra was the king of deities (*dev*).

29. Jambavati was wife of Krishna. Samba was her son.
30. Jaydrath was the king of Sindhu and brother in law of Duryodhana, married to Dushala, only sister of one hundred Kauravas.
31. Karna was the eldest son of Kunti who left him as she gave birth to him before marriage, brought up by Adhirath (a charioteer) and Radha. He was a great warrior who was befriended by Duryodhana looking at his strength and valour.
32. Kripacharya was the guru (teacher) of Pandavas and Kauravas and a council member of Kuru kingdom.
33. Krishna was son of Vasudev and Devaki, brought up by Nand and Yashoda and an incarnation of Lord Vishnu.
34. Kritvarma was a Yadav commander who had taken away gem of Satrajit (father of Satyabhama) and disliked Krishna after he married to Satyabhama.
35. Kunti was wife of Pandu and mother of Pandavas.
36. Kuntibhoj was father of Kunti.
37. Kuru was a legendary king in India whose descendants were known as Kauravas. To differentiate two sides of a family of king Dhritrashtra and Pandu, the sons of Dhritrashtra are known as Kauravas and of Pandu as Pandavas.
38. Kurukshetra is the place where Mahabharat was fought. At present, it is in Haryana state of India.
39. Mahabharat war is a war fought between Pandavas and Kauravas in Kurukshetra in which almost all the kings and warriors of that period participated.
40. Markandeya was a great sage.
41. Nandini, a cow, was the daughter of most sacred Kamdhenu cow.
42. Pandavas were sons of king Pandu, younger son of Vichitravirya and brother of Dhritrashtra. Pandu was

made king of Hastinapur as his elder brother Dhritrashtra was blind. He had two wives as Kunti and Madri. Kunti had four sons i.e. Karna, Yudhishthir, Bhima, and Arjun while Madri two as Nakul and Sahdeva. Kunti left Karna immediately after the birth. Pandu's sons Yudhishthir, Bhima, Arjun, Nakul and Sahdeva were called Pandavas.

43. Nakul was son of Pandu and Madri.
44. Pandu was son of Shantanu and Satyavati who married to Kunti and Madri.
45. Parashuram was a sage and great warrior, said to be incarnation of Lord Vishnu.
46. Purujit was brother of Kunti, mother of Pandavas and son of king Kuntibhoj.
47. Rukmini was wife of Krishna. Rukmi was her brother.
48. Samba was son of Krishna from Jambavati. Pradumn was Krishna's son from Rukmini.
49. Saibya was the king of Suvira, a great archer, whose daughter was married to Akrur, a chieftain of Yadav's army.
50. Sahdeva was the younger son of Pandu and Madri.
51. Sanatkumars are sages and sons of Lord Brahma, the creator of the universe.
52. Satyaki was a Yadav chieftain and fought from the side of Pandavas.
53. Shalv was the king of Saubha and brother of Madri.
54. Shishupal was a relative and cousin of Krishna who disliked him.
55. Shursen was father of Vasudev and grandfather of Krishna.
56. Subhadra was daughter of Vasudev and Rohini. Vasudev was father of Lord Krishna.
57. Shakuni was brother of Gandhari.

58. Shantanu was from Kuru dynasty and king of Hastinapur. He married to Ganga and Satyavati.
59. Shukracharya was Guru of Rakshas.
60. Subala was the king of Gandhar and father of Shakuni and Gandhari.
61. Uttara was wife of Abhimanyu. Kumar Uttar was his brother.
62. Vashishtha was a great sage and one of the Saptrishi having divine powers. He had a cow named Nandini.
63. Vasudev was father of Krishna.
64. Vayu was the deity of air.
65. Vichitravirya was son of Shantanu and Satyavati. Chitrangad was his elder brother.
66. Vidur was the prime minister of Dhritrashtra and paternal uncle of Kauravas and Pandavas.
67. Vikarna was brother of Duryodhana.
68. Virat was the king of Matsa kingdom and father in law of Abhimanyu, son of Arjun and Subhadra.
69. Yudhishthir was the eldest son of Pandu and Kunti.
70. Yudhumanyu and Uttamaujas were brothers of Drupad.

CHAPTER TWO

Bhishma leaves the throne of Hastinapur

Devavrat was the son of king Shantanu of Hastinapur from Kuru dynasty who was known later as Bhishma. His mother's name was Ganga hence also known as *Gangaputra*. Though eight sons were born from them, he was the only son lived for long as Shantanu prevented Ganga from putting new born baby into river Ganga.

Once Shantanu saw a beautiful woman on the banks of river Ganga and fell in love with her. He proposed her for the marriage. The girl was Ganga herself. She agreed to his proposal with a condition that he would not ask any question about her actions even if not liked by him. She further told if he would ask it, she would leave him. Once Shantanu agreed, they married.

Shantanu and Ganga continued enjoying married life. When their first son was born, queen Ganga took him to river Ganga and put in the water. The child disappeared in Ganga river after getting drowned. This way seven children were put in the water by queen Ganga and they all disappeared in the river. Due to the promise, Shantanu could not question her action. When eighth son was born and queen Ganga took him to the river, Shantanu followed and stopped her from putting new born baby in the river. He asked her the reason of performing such a cruel action of drowning their babies in the river. Queen Ganga reminded his promise and told that he should have not questioned her action. Since he had broken the promise, she would have to leave. Shantanu insisted her to tell the reason of drowning their babies into the river.

Queen Ganga agreed and told that she was in the human form of river Ganga and had given the birth to eight *Vasus* (Attendants of Lord Indra). Eight *Vasus* were cursed by sage Vashishth for taking birth in the mortal form as one of them was involved in stealing his cow Nandini and others had protected him. Such an action was against *dharma* and undesirable for the deities. Sage Vashishth cursed seven Vasus to take birth for a short period and return to their place but the eighth will have to live for a longer period on earth as he was directly involved in the undesired action. Those *vasus* have taken birth from us and I have sent seven of them to their place but eighth will have to live longer now. She told that she would hand over eighth child to him when he becomes young. Thereafter, she disappeared with the baby. Thereafter, she brought him up and got trained from Guru Brahaspati, Shukracharya, Vashishtha, Chyavana, Sanatkumar, Markandeya, Parashuram and Indra. Later, she handed over him to Shantanu. This child was named as Devavrat.

Devavrat was the heir of king Shantanu, being the only son and Shantanu also wanted to hand over the reign of Hastinapur to him. Public of Hastinapur also loved him as he was kind, intelligent and a great warrior.

Remember, things do not go as per the wishes of a king, father, mother or public. It is the destiny which matters and the destiny or God had prescribed something else for

Devavrat.

One day, Shantanu went to forest and saw a woman named Satyavati, from the community of fishermen. He fell in love with her and made a proposal for the marriage to his father. Her father, the headman of fishing community told that he would agree to the proposal provided the king declaring would be son of Satyavati as his heir. Shantanu knew that Devavrat has the right to become his successor as king of Hastinapur so did not agree to the condition and returned to the palace still thinking about Satyavati. Since the king neglected royal affairs and looked in grief, Devavrat tried to know the reason behind it.

It is very difficult to hide love even in case of great people.

Knowing the reason that his father was in love with the daughter of head of fishermen, he went to him and requested to agree to the proposal of his father. Satyavati's father told his condition to Devavrat. Devavrat immediately agreed and ceded his right to the throne and promised to protect the throne of Hastinapur in place of becoming the king.

Satyavati's father wanted to make sure that Hastinapur is ruled by the sons of Satyavati and their descendants so expressed his doubt to Devavrat that even if he ceded his right, his sons might claim it.

Then Devavrat vowed that he would not marry lifelong so there is no question of his sons. Due to such a strong and firm vow, he was named as Bhishma.

Destiny changed the legal right made by the kings that elder son will only be made successor of the king.

Satyavati's father was a human being and did not know about the future. He was not knowing that he had sown the seed of Mahabharat war in which all the descendants of Satyavati and Shantanu will be standing in the battlefield of Kurukshetra for killing themselves in future. He was not aware that his condition of Satyavati's marriage will lead to Mahabharat war. Probably, if Devavrat could have been made king, Mahabharat war probably could have been avoided.

Even Bhishma who was the reincarnation of *Vasu* did not know that his vow of attachment to the throne will lead to helplessness in witnessing *adharma* and sinful activities.

Remember Chapter 4 of Bhagwadgita, Lord Krishna telling Arjun that I am aware of my births and also yours but not you. Although, birthless, immortal and immutable I appear and reappear whenever and wherever *dharma* (Godly activities) declines and rise of *adharma* is predominant to protect devotees of *dharma* and eradication of those involved in sinful activities.

Remember if Bhishma was the king of Hastinapur, Mahabharat war could not have been fought. Probably if Bhishma could not have vowed for the attachment to the throne of Hastinapur, he would not have sided to Dhritrashtra who was the king and then Dhritrashtra or Duryodhana could not have dared to go for war. But it is the destiny which prevails. God is the doer, not the human beings even if humans boast of master of their actions.

Nevertheless, Shantanu and Satyavati got married and Chitrangad and Vichitravirya were born from such marriage.

Satyavati's father might have become happy as he was sure that Hastinapur would be ruled by his generations. Let's see what happened to next generation.

After the death of Shantanu, Chitrangad was made the king of Hastinapur. In a short period, Chitrangad was killed by a gandharva. Now, the hope was in Vichitravirya only.

After the death of Chitrangad, Vichitravirya was crowned the king of Hastinapur.

CHAPTER THREE

Bhishma was a great warrior, wise and knowledgeable. He had vowed to remain attached to the throne of Hastinapur and never broke it. The kings during that period knew that it was impossible for them to defeat Bhishma so they had no choice but to agree to him on all accounts.

Satyavati wanted to marry his son Vichitravirya. Just then, king of Kashi arranged a swayamvar for her three daughters named Amba, Ambika and Ambalika. In a swayamvar, girl was free to choose anyone for the marriage as per her choice. Sometimes, particular condition was kept from the bride side which was required to be fulfilled by the aspiring grooms for the marriage. Normally such conditions were to test wisdom or strength of the aspiring grooms.

Bhishma went to the swayamvar, not for participating in it but to abduct the girls. It is not known why Vichitravirya was not sent by Satyavati. Possible reason maybe that the kings might not be giving him same status as of Kshatriya kings because of Satyavati's background. Maybe, due to the same reason there could be a fear of him not getting chosen by the princesses. Such a situation might have been humiliation for Hastinapur king. Not sure about the reason but Bhishma was sent to abduct the girls and bring them to Hastinapur so that Vichitravirya's marriage could be solemnized at Hastinapur.

As Bhishma was attached to the throne, he went to Kashi and challenged the princes and kings assembled in the swayamvar to stop him or allow to take away the princesses to Hastinapur for the marriage of his step brother Vichitravirya. Even though this was an act of abduction, most of the kings and princes did not show any resistance except king Shalv.

Actually, Shalv loved Amba and she had already decided that she would choose him her groom in the swayamvar. So Shalv tried to stop Bhishma but was overpowered by Bhishma, unaware of their relation. Bhishma abducted all three princesses and took them to Hastinapur for the marriage with Vichitravirya. When reached Hastinapur, Amba disclosed her intention of marrying to Shalv acknowledging she loved him. Bhishma sent Amba to Shalv but then he refused to marry her saying that he was defeated by Bhishma as such had no right to marry her now.

King Shalv had felt insulted on his defeat from Bhishma. Maybe, he felt humiliated from Amba for not disclosing her love when Bhishma was abducting her. Though he knew that Amba was neither married nor loved anyone other than him but insult prevailed over his consciousness.

Remember, later Shalv's sister was married to Pandu, son of Vichitravirya and he wanted his sister's sons made heirs of Hastinapur but that also did not materialize. King Shalv fought from Kauravas' side during Mahabharat war.

CHAPTER FOUR

Amba had approached to Shalv and was sure that he would marry her but on his refusal, she was nowhere so decided to return to Hastinapur. She felt that Bhishma was the root cause of her nightmare.

On return to Hastinapur, she requested Bhishma to marry her as he had abducted her and won in the fight with Shalv. But Bhishma refused saying neither he had abducted her for himself nor was aware of her relation with Shalv. He had abducted her for Vichitravirya so he can marry her. But Vichitravirya also refused saying that she loved to Shalv so he would not marry her. Now, Amba's last hope was shattered but was helpless. So, she tried to get justice by approaching to the kings of powerful states but they refused to arbitrate as they were afraid of Bhishma.

Finally, Amba was exhausted and felt insulted. Getting no help from any corner, she tried to take revenge herself from Bhishma by getting boon from the sages and deities. She was sure that Bhishma alone was responsible for her misery and insult.

Amba took all the steps including austerities to please sages, deities and Lord. She left home with a mission to take revenge of her insult from Bhishma. From the penance of Amba, Lord was pleased and asked her to demand a boon. Adamant for the revenge from Bhishma, she desired to be born as a man capable to slay Bhishma. God blessed her that she would become a man in her next birth and will be responsible for the death of Bhishma. Getting such a boon, she created a funeral pyre of wood on the bank of the river Yamuna and jumped into the fire for taking rebirth. After all, she wanted to take revenge as early as possible.

Lord Krishna told in Bhagwadgita in Chapter 8: one who is able to remember Me at the time of death achieves my gesture. One remembers at the time of death what has been absorbed through continued contemplation. Amba had absorbed revenge from Bhishma through continued contemplation and as such it continued during her rebirth also as wisdom and temperaments transform into new body from previous birth and same was the case of Amba.

CHAPTER FIVE

Drupad was the king of Panchal but was not having children. So he started austerities for getting the blessings of Lord Shiva. Lord Shiva granted him the boon. He was also told that he could get a girl child whose gender will get transformed into a boy later. Drupad had no clue of its reason though it was due to destiny. And then destiny always prevails.

Drupad got a daughter who was named as Shikhandini but he started calling her Shikhandi knowing that her gender would be transformed.

Actually, Amba was born as Drupad's daughter. Drupad brought her up as a boy but Bhishma had received the news of the girl child, named Shikhandini.

Dhrupad married Shikhandi with the daughter of Hiranyavarna, the king of Dasharna in the garb of a boy but her identity got revealed after the marriage. Feeling cheated, Hiranyavarna declared war with Drupad. Distressed by the turn of events, Shikhandini went to the forest and sat on fast unto death. A *yaksha* (a deity) named SthunaKarna saved her and offered his own male gender in exchange to Shikhandini's female gender. After this, Shikhandini became male Shikhandi.

Thereafter, Shikhandi was accepted as a male though Bhishma continued considering him as a female.

No one could think that Shikhandini or even as Shikhandi can harm Bhishma or would be the cause of death of Bhishma except Lord Krishna who was incarnation of God. Who knew that Amba, reborn as Shikhandini and transformed into Shikhandi will be used for the death of Bhishma, the greatest warrior of that period during Mahabharat war.

In Chapter 7 of Bhagwadgita, Lord Krishna told Arjun about His knowing the past, present and future of every living entity however no one knows his or her past and future.

And Lord Krishna knew the past and future of Shikhandi and Bhishma.

CHAPTER SIX

Vichitravirya had married to Ambika and Ambalika. He ruled Hastinapur for few years but died due to tuberculosis.

Look at the destiny: Hastinapur was without a king within a short period.

Lord Krishna has said in Bhagwadgita that He only knows past and future. A lot was still to come in future.

As Vichitravirya died without children, Kuru dynasty was at the risk of extinction. Satyavati's father wanted children of Satyavati to be heirs of the king Shantanu ruling Hastinapur. Look to the destiny that her husband, and her sons were all dead.

And, Satyavati had no one to be crowned as the king of Hastinapur during her life itself.

Finding no option, Satyavati tried to convince Bhishma to agree for his marriage so that there was a successor of the king of Hastinapur but Bhishma refused the proposal and reiterated his vow.

Satyavati then called *Rishi* Vyas, her first child and asked him to perform *Niyoga* to impregnate her daughters-in-laws. It is said that Ambika closed her eyes looking to *Rishi* Vyas and Ambika got frightened looking at him.

Thus, Dhritrashtra was born blind from Ambika, and Pandu weak from Ambalika.

Lord Krishna told Arjun in Bhagwadgita in Chapter 3: As ignorant perform action with the desire to its result, knowledgeable should perform action for the welfare of the world. All the actions are influenced by the senses in the material world and ignorant get attached to them thinking themselves as the doer of the actions. But a knowledgeable knows about the doer and performs virtuous action without desire of the result of the action.

Satyavati's father performed action with the desire to its result. Lord Krishna told Arjun to perform all the actions for the welfare of others. When one performs action with the material desires or with the attachment to the desire of its result, his action is of vileness temperament.

Bhishma was attached to the throne so continued to protect it and arranged training for Dhritrashtra and Pandu.

Dhritrashtra, being blind was denied to become the king and Pandu was declared the king of Hastinapur.

It is anybody's guess what Dhritrashtra might have felt: frustrated, depressed or insulted - God knows.

CHAPTER SEVEN

Dhritrashtra was blind by birth but Satyavati wanted to solemnize his marriage. Hastinapur was very rich and powerful kingdom as Bhishma was protecting it. No king in India had courage to defy Bhishma's proposal.

Bhishma sent proposal for the marriage of Dhritrashtra to Subala, the king of Gandhar with his daughter Gandhari. Subala had no choice but to accept the proposal as he could not reject the proposal of Bhishma. Shakuni, brother of Gandhari did not like it and felt humiliated by the proposal of Bhishma as he had sent the proposal of a blind prince for Gandhari. When Gandhari came to know about blindness of Dhritrashtra, she decided to blindfold herself in order to be like her husband. Some feel that the act was due to her love and dedication to Dhritrashtra and some are of view that it was an act of protest against Bhishma.

Thereafter, Bhishma arranged Pandu's marriage with Kunti, the adoptive daughter of Kuntibhoj and daughter of Shursen. Shursen was father of Vasudev thus grandfather of Krishna. Kunti was thus aunt (*Bua*) of Krishna.

Pandu was an excellent archer and a great warrior.

Bhishma went to the king of Madra and asked the hand of Madri, sister of Shalv for Pandu. King of Madra was not in favour of relation with Kuru dynasty but had no courage to reject the proposal. Bhishma took Madri for Pandu and thus Pandu married to Madri also.

Despite Dhritrashtra being the elder was denied the throne because of his blindness. One can guess his feelings as he might be waiting for the same from the childhood after all as per the custom, eldest son was declared successor of the king. And Bhishma was already protecting Hastinapur. Who knows whether he waited his younger brother to deny the throne for him. When Pandu accepted it, God only knows about Dhritrashtra's feelings, the feelings of joy, humiliation or frustration.

CHAPTER EIGHT

Pandu was crowned the king of Hastinapur even though younger to Dhritrashtra. The reason of Dhritrashtra not being made the king was his blindness only. Dhritrashtra was adjudged incapable to become the king.

But destiny is supreme and no one at that time imagined that one day he would still become the king. Only God knew the future.

Pandu became the king of Hastinapur and started ruling. Once, Pandu saw a couple of deer in the forest. Even though the couple was in the process of coitus, Pandu shot arrows at them. Suddenly, he heard human voice and then came to know that it was *Rishi* Kindama and his wife, making love in the form of deer.

He argued with *Rishi* Kindama of his right of hunting and was not regretful of his action. The dying sage cursed to Pandu because he had not only killed them in the midst of lovemaking even in the form of deer but was not regretful of his action. He cursed him that he would die if approached for making love.

Mind thinks about material desires as they either gratify own senses or are attached to those one has attachment. King Pandu had no children at this stage and was cursed for death if he intended to make love. In such conditions, one even thinks of renunciation.

King Pandu probably bent towards renunciation and renounced his position and went to the forest with Kunti and Madri. Dhritrashtra was made the de facto king. Same Dhritrashtra who was blind and was declared unsuitable for the throne some time back. God only knows past, present and future. Lord Krishna says that ignorant do not agree to the existence of God.

If Duryodhana could have taken birth by this time, probably there would have been no Mahabharat war as he would have been the eldest but something else was hidden in the future.

Pandu had left the palace and gone to the forest with his wives Kunti and Madri. By now, Kunti and Madri also knew about the curse. One day, Pandu told to Kunti that he also desired to have his sons and she told him a secret.

Kunti had so far not told the secret of knowing child-bearing *mantra* granted to her by sage Durvasa with which she could invite the deities and bear the children. She had already tested it once by inviting deity *Surya* (Sun) before her marriage but never told to anyone about the son including Pandu.

Pandu was overjoyed to know from Kunti about the *mantra* and asked her to use it. He suggested to invite *Dharmaraj*, *Vayu* and *Indra*. Kunti did so and thus Yudhishthir, Bhima and Arjun were born. But, destiny was supreme as Yudhishthir was born before Duryodhana and thus became the eldest. Bhima was born on the same day as Duryodhana. Probably if Yudhishthir was not there, Duryodhana could have claimed to be the eldest even though it is said that Bhima was only few moments older than Duryodhana.

Pandu then asked Kunti to share *mantra* of inviting deities to Madri and on inviting Ashwin Kumars, Madri gave birth to Nakul and Sahdeva.

Even though death is certain but Pandu knew the cause of his death. One day, Pandu insisted Madri for sexual intercourse and then died. Probably, he had no desire to live.

It is said that no one knows about the death as it may come any day. But we do not know that many of us invite death when fed up of living. Sometimes, few people wish death of their near ones on their behalf.

Whatever may be the reason, Pandu had died even after knowing the curse. His body was cremated in the forest itself. Sad due to sudden happening, Madri took her own life after handing over her children to Kunti. Kunti considered all five children as her own and these were known as Pandavas, sons of Pandu.

In the palace, Gandhari gave birth to 101 children - 100 boys and one girl named Dushala. Duryodhana was the eldest. They were called Kauravas to differentiate between sons of Dhritrashtra and Pandu. Kauravas mean the descendants of Kuru as such Pandavas and Kauravas, all were Kauravas, the descendants of Kuru.

Dhritrashtra continued only the de facto king.

And Pandavas and Kauravas grew up with the desire of getting throne of Hastinapur. Pandavas wanted it for Yudhishthir and Kauravas for Duryodhana.

And Duryodhana might have been under the impression that Yudhishthir will claim the throne of Hastinapur. All Pandavas were united and remained together and had affinity among them hence Duryodhana developed hate for his cousins, only for the power.

CHAPTER NINE

After the death of Pandu and Madri, Kunti returned to Hastinapur. Kripacharya started giving training to Pandavas and Kauravas.

Bhishma was still protecting Hastinapur even though Dhritrashtra was the de facto king. He was looking to someone who could make children great warriors.

Shakuni had felt humiliated when Bhishma had sent proposal of Dhritrashtra's marriage for his sister Gandhari. He now wanted that Hastinapur should be ruled by his nephew i.e. Gandhari's son Duryodhana. Probably, he also had ambition to rule Hastinapur through Duryodhana so he came to Hastinapur and started moulding Duryodhana as per his choice. He knew that Duryodhana will not be made the king of Hastinapur as Dhritrashtra was only a defacto king. As Pandu had become the king, his elder son maybe declared his successor. Further, Yudhishthir was elder to Duryodhana and as such Bhishma might even say that the eldest in Pandavas and Kauravas will be the king. So, he started manipulating the children affairs as he could guess the behavior and thirst of throne in Duryodhana.

It is said that Shakuni wanted to destroy Hastinapur as he felt humiliated and insulted from Bhishma's proposal of Gandhari's marriage though maybe he wanted to destroy Pandavas and his supporters and then take on others. Thus, his first target were Pandavas.

Bhima was very powerful and mighty compared to other Pandavas. So, Duryodhana and Shakuni thought of eliminating Bhima first. They tried to kill Bhima multiple times, even by poisoning and throwing him into a river but was rescued by *Nāgas*.

Nevertheless, Pandavas could not be eliminated and they continued their training. Kripacharya, in addition of royal affairs, was training to Pandavas and Kauravas but Bhishma wanted a guru who could devote full time with them and teach all the subjects.

Look to the destiny, Dronacharya himself entered Hastinapur with his motive.

CHAPTER TEN

Dron and Drupad had studied together in the *ashram* of sage Bhardwaj, Drona's father. They became close friends and shared their belongings during stay in the *ashram*. Once, Drupad told Dron that on becoming king, he would share half of his kingdom with him. After the study, they got parted. Dhrupad became king, while Drona became *acharya* (Guru) and lived a miserable life of poverty even unable to feed to his son properly.

Dronacharya decided to take help from king Drupad as he was his close friend during *ashram* days. When he approached Drupad for help, he refused, maybe he thought of Dronacharya asking half of the kingdom. He told him the difference between a king and petitioner. When Dronacharya reminded him what he said in the *ashram*, he humiliated him narrating difference of the status between a king and beggar. Dronacharya felt insulted as he had called him beggar and vowed for the revenge.

Dronacharya thought of the kingdom able to fight with Panchal and understood that it could only be Hastinapur. Assured that it was only the kingdom of Hastinapur who could defeat Drupad, he went to Hastinapur with a mission of defeating Drupad and asking him for the apology.

In Hastinapur, Bhishma also wanted a guru for Pandavas and Kauravas. And there could be no guru better than Dronacharya that time.

Soon destiny arranged the meeting of Bhishma and Dronacharya.

Dronacharya went to Hastinapur. Bhishma came to know his presence in Hastinapur when he heard about his act of taking out a ball from a well with the help of straws from the children, he invited Dronacharya and appointed him royal trainer.

And thus, Dronacharya became trainer of Pandavas and Kauravas.

As Dronacharya wanted to take revenge from Drupad, he ensured that no one else get training who can defeat his disciples to enable him to prepare children for taking revenge of his insult.

CHAPTER ELEVEN

Dronacharya started imparting training to the princes with a mission of taking revenge from, Drupad rather insult him and training as secondary objective being part of his duty.

Dronacharya gave training to all the princes and understood soon that Arjun was the best student and if trained properly, would be able to defeat Drupad. He started giving special training to him keeping in mind that he was able to defeat Drupad.

Arjun was an intelligent and dedicated trainee who wanted to learn as much as he could. And, Dronacharya gave him all types of training he was aware.

Looking to the dedication and learning of Arjun, Dronacharya understood that the moment of his fulfilling the goal was close by.

When the training was complete, Dronacharya asked the princes to fight with Drupad, capture him and bring to him which will be the gift to their guru. First all the Kauravas attacked Drupad, but he defeated them. Then Pandavas led by Arjun went and defeated Drupad. Drupad was brought to Dronacharya by Arjun in ropes as per his directions.

Dronacharya was waiting for this moment and told to Arjun to free him and give half the kingdom of Panchal in alms retaining half of the kingdom.

Drupad, king of Panchal was thus insulted by Dronacharya and Drupad and his relatives waited for the opportunity to take revenge of his insult from Dronacharya.

Opportunity which came in the form of Mahabharat war.

CHAPTER TWELVE

Pandavas were getting popularity in the public due to their intelligence, courage and ethical behavior but this was against the plan of Duryodhana and Shakuni. So they planned a crooked plot to eliminate all the Pandavas at a time.

Duryodhana asked Purochana, one of his confidents to design and execute a palatial guest house on the river bank which can catch fire at a faster rate. He designed and constructed a beautiful structure named *Lakshagriha*, made of inflammable materials like lacquer and wax.

Once ready, Duryodhana revealed everyone that he had constructed a beautiful guest house on the river bank and would like brother Yudhishthir to stay in it with his brothers and aunt Kunti first. It was located in the forest, full of natural beauty even though it was constructed as a death trap for Pandavas, looking like an accident.

Shakuni and Duryodhana had built it secretly with a motive but Vidur could know about it during construction when considerable inflammable material was being transported to the site in place of durable and fire resistant material. Further, construction was directly being supervised by Shakuni and Duryodhana, which was also unusual. When Vidur sent his spy, he came to know about the plot. Vidur understood that the guest house might have been planned for Pandavas so he got constructed a tunnel near the guest house connected to it, entry of which was closed.

When Duryodhana requested Pandavas to enjoy living in the beautiful guest house, they agreed to. When Duryodhana was bidding farewell to Pandavas, Vidur advised to Yudhishthir in code words to use the tunnel during fire and thus warned Pandavas about the danger. Reaching to the guest house, Pandavas tried to decode the words what Vidur had said and understood soon that the place was built to eliminate them.

Pandavas guarded the palace till they could locate the tunnel and were ready to exit. Once ready, they pretended to be neglecting security. Duryodhana had asked Purochana to fire the place and simultaneously made arrangements to burn him in the fire to ensure that he was not able to disclose the secret to anyone else. When Pandavas saw him coming to fire the place, Pandavas themselves put it on fire and escaped through the tunnel along with their mother Kunti.

Though Pandavas escaped, they went on hiding themselves simultaneously building relations with locals.

Shakuni and Duryodhana have not even spared Kunti, mother of Pandavas hence Pandavas also might have thought about taking revenge from Duryodhana.

CHAPTER THIRTEEN

News reached to Hastinapur regarding the guest house gutted in the fire in which Pandavas were staying. Everyone was shocked from the death of Pandavas except Kauravas, Shakuni and Vidur. Though Kauravas and Shakuni were expressing sadness but were delighted from the successful execution of their plan. Vidur was not showing any concern as he knew that Pandavas have escaped.

Time passed.

Pandavas reached Panchal when Draupadi's swayamvar was being held. Pandavas went to the *swayamvar* dressed as *Brahmans* and sat to see the proceedings. The test was to shoot an arrow to pierce the eye of a golden fish by looking at its reflection in the oil, filled up in a vessel.

Many kings and princes were attending the *swayamvar* including Duryodhana and Karna. Krishna was also present in the *swayamvar*, but not as an aspiring groom.

At the *swayamvar*, kings and princes were unable to pass the test. Karna was a great archer. As he walked towards the bow to take the aim, Draupadi stopped him and denied marrying to the son of a charioteer. Karna was brought up by a charioteer and was considered his son. Feeling insulted, Karna returned to his seat.

Then Arjun went towards the bow, aimed towards the fish and pierced it.

On Arjun succeeding in the test, the kings and princes including Kauravas and Karna protested, raising the issue of his caste. Lord Krishna then defended the decision of Brahman boy as he had aimed when all the kshatriyas had failed.

Lord Krishna recognized Arjun and other Pandavas. Kauravas, Karna and other kshatriya kings were aware that Panchal was a strong kingdom and didn't want to go too far which could take ugly turn leading to war.

But Karna felt insulted from this incident as Draupadi had refused to marry him even though he was a great archer and could make the aim.

Soon Pandavas' identity was known to Drupad so also to others. When Bhishma heard about them, he advised Dhritrashtra to call them to Hastinapur. Dhritrashtra called them and divided the kingdom of Hastinapur to end the dispute between Pandavas and Kauravas.

CHAPTER FOURTEEN

Dhritrashtra chose to divide kingdom in a way that Pandavas get the land which was not very fertile. Even some of it was under possession of *Naga* kings who almost had independence. This area was called Khandavprasth where Takshak, king of *Naga* dynasty was ruling. He lived there with other tribes like *Pisacha, Rakshasas, Daityas and Danavas*. Arjun set fire in Khandavprasth which was full of trees of semi-arid region for the development of the area. *Naga* chief Takshak was out of his place but his son Aswasena was present. Aswasena and Mayasur escaped from the forest when the fire broke out. Thus, Khandavprasth was made ready for the development.

However, Aswasena and Takshak felt humiliated from the attack of Arjun who set fire in their place. Aswasena tried to take revenge during Mahabharat war from Arjun. Takshak tried to take revenge but succeeded only during the period of Parikshit, grandson of Arjun after Pandavas had left for heaven.

Nevertheless, Pandavas worked hard and developed barren Khandavprasth into a beautiful city renaming it as Indraprastha (present Delhi) and made their capital. It is said, Pandavas were given *Sonipat, Panipat, Baghpat* and *Tilpat* in addition to Khandavprasth thereby area surrounding five villages. Since, Pandavas had relations to deities, they could take their help. Vishwakarma, architect of deity Indra is said to have designed and built

Indraprastha in barren land housing a grand palace, wide roads, lush green gardens, water elements, and other beautiful structures.

Mayasur also contributed in its design and built beautiful convention centre known as *Maya Sabha* or the Hall of Illusions, with reflective crystal floors looking like pools of water. The royal palace was not only designed beautifully but also built with splendorous and mysterious materials having flowing water lines, magnificent halls, pools and grand meeting rooms.

Pandavas had made their capital in Indraprastha and wanted to show its grandeur with their power so decided to organize *Rajsuya yajna* to achieve sovereignty and status. Bhishma also supported it.

Bhishma attended the ceremony with Kauravas. Yudhishthir was to be crowned of Indraprastha. Bhishma suggested Yudhishthir to give Krishna the highest place in the ceremony.

Remember, splendorous palaces, buildings or infrastructure are liked if made for the welfare of common people. If these are made for individuals or owned by the kings, they are not liked particularly by those of equal ranks. Similar was the condition of Shakuni and Duryodhana.

Indraprastha was ready to receive kings from all over the country and Pandavas were on top of the roof as Yudhishthir's coronation was being held along with *Rajsuya yajna* to show their supremacy.

The ceremony was to commence and everything appeared to be under control. But no one knew what was hidden in the future except God.

Shishupal was also invited in the coronation ceremony as he was a relative of Hastinapur king. He was also a relative of Krishna but disliked him due to Rukmini marrying to him. Rukmini was sister of Rukmi, prince of Vidarbha, who wanted to marry his sister to Shishupal but Krishna married to Rukmini. Shishupal felt insulted and started hating Lord Krishna.

When Shishupal saw Krishna being given highest status and worshipped, he started abusing and insulting Lord Krishna. Lord Krishna forgave one hundred abuses and thereafter slayed him.

Thereafter, no one opposed Pandavas.

The ceremony started. Duryodhana was taking gifts from the visitors on behalf of Pandavas and was amazed to see the expensive gifts.

After the ceremony, while visiting splendorous and mysterious palace Duryodhana fell prey to the illusions. When he stepped on the apparently looking beautiful crystal floor of the courtyard, he fell into water body. Incidentally, Draupadi saw him falling in the water body from the balcony, and started laughing and jokingly called him blind son of blind father.

And Duryodhana felt so insulted that he left Indraprastha thereafter with his brothers and Shakuni for Hastinapur to take revenge of his insult.

Mahabharat war started knocking the door.

CHAPTER FIFTEEN

Duryodhana, Dushashan and Karna insult to Pandavas and Draupadi

Duryodhana had left Indraprastha feeling insulted from the Draupadi's laughing, calling him blind son of a blind father and probably disgraced by the glory of Pandavas. Shakuni had also witnessed the incidence so flared the incidence. After all, words are sharper than sword.

Duryodhana wanted to take revenge of his insult even by direct fight with Pandavas but Shakuni prevented him and suggested to take revenge from the weakness of Yudhishthir. Shakuni knew that it was not possible to defeat Pandavas in war at this stage as many kings had accepted the power of Yudhishthir so advised Duryodhana to adopt a deceiving trick.

Shakuni knew that Yudhishthir was fond of gambling but was no match to him as Shakuni was the master of the game of dice and could throw them as per his sweet will. It is said that he had full control on the dices he had.

Shakuni wanted to ensure that Yudhishthir accepted invitation to come to Hastinapur and agreed to play. For the same, he wanted Yudhishthir to be invited by someone to whom he would not refuse. Then the timing was to be perfect so he accepted the invitation without fail. He also knew that Krishna would never allow him to accept such invitation so he asked Duryodhana to wait and send invitation after Krishna had left Indraprastha.

When Shakuni got the news of Krishna's departure from Indraprastha, he asked Duryodhana to pursue his father Dhritrashtra to invite Yudhishthir to Hastinapur for a family get together to celebrate the success of *Rajsuya yajna* by playing dice before elders and gurus for the celebration. Dhritrashtra invited Yudhishthir and got him trapped in the plot of Shakuni.

Pandavas with their mother Kunti and Draupadi reached Hastinapur where Duryodhana gave rousing welcome to Pandavas. Next day Duryodhana personally went to receive them in the guest house and brought them to the palace where Dhritrashtra, Bhishma, Karna, Vidur, Dronacharya and other dignitaries were present.

When Yudhishthir had taken the seat, Duryodhana told him that uncle Shakuni would throw dice on his behalf and he would keep the stakes. Yudhishthir was trapped and knew that he was no match to Shakuni still continued thinking it was unethical to get up from the seat however gambling itself was unethical. Shakuni was happy looking to Yudhishthir getting trapped. Shakuni had defeated Yudhishthir even before the play started by controlling his mind.

As the play started, plan of Shakuni was getting executed. Yudhishthir behaved like an ordinary gambler forgetting that he was a king and a family man. He went on keeping stakes of money, jewels, land, and then the kingdom and lost all. He even put on stake his brothers as they were his property, on provocation of Duryodhana and lost them also. He did not stop there and put him also on stake and lost. Thereafter, on further provocation of Duryodhana, put Draupadi on stake and lost her too.

Duryodhana was overjoyed, crazy to take revenge, revenge of glory exhibited by Pandavas in Indraprastha during coronation of Yudhishthir and revenge of insult done by Draupadi.

And he publically called Pandavas as his slaves.

Then Karna told him that slaves had no right to wear royal accessories and have weapons as such their royal accessories and weapons should be snatched.

Duryodhana and Karna snatched royal accessories and weapons from Pandavas thus insulted them before the dignitaries, family members and general public.

But, that was not all. Duryodhana then thought of taking revenge from Draupadi by insulting her in public.

Duryodhana asked his brother Dushashan to bring Draupadi in the court. When Draupadi refused to come there from the palace, Dushashan brought her dragging by her hair to the court.

The scene of dragging a queen, a sister in law, a lady and a guest was horrible and beyond imagination. Queen of a king who had just been crowned was being dragged before her husbands. A daughter in law was being dragged before her father in law and grandfather in law. A sister in law was being dragged before her brothers in laws and by a brother in law. This ghastly act was being performed before family members, courtiers, dignitaries of Hastinapur, courtiers and common public.

Though most of them were ashamed to see her being dragged that too by someone who was her own brother in law, they did not dare to speak even a single word before Duryodhana due to fear. Draupadi looked around and saw Pandavas keeping their heads down and unable to see her eye to eye. She then saw to Bhishma, Dronacharya and other elders sitting there and asked why they were silent but got no reply from them too. Then, she announced that she was being insulted by everyone present there either directly or by witnessing ghastly act so they would have to pay the price for the sin they were committing by keeping silence.

Duryodhana was not only insulting Draupadi but committing a great blunder and heinous crime much larger than anyone else having done in the history for which Duryodhana had to pay heavily in future and had to be designated as an evil man in the history.

Blinded by the win in the gamble and strong desire of revenge, Duryodhana asked Dushashan to remove her sari (attire) and make her sit on his thigh.

Winning in gamble is like becoming monstrous.

Bhima was boiling looking to the insult of Draupadi. Suddenly, he shouted and vowed that one day he would break the thigh of Duryodhana.

Draupadi told to the elders that it was shame on all those calling themselves kshatriyas, the descendants of *Bharat* and still being part of insulting their own daughter in law by witnessing a heinous crime silently. And for such a crime, they will have to face befitting reply in future.

And Duryodhana, Karna and their friends laughed on her helplessness shamelessly. They asked Dushashan to go ahead to remove her *sari* to make her naked. As Dushashan approached for removing her *sari*, Bhima vowed again that he would break Dushashan's heart.

Draupadi then remembered Lord Krishna for her help who had promised her to protect whenever she was in trouble. Lord Krishna came there and helped Draupadi remaining himself invisible. Dushashan failed to remove her *sari.*

Draupadi untied her hair and vowed that she would tie her hair only after washing them from Dushashan's blood.

Dhritrashtra realized now that there could be major problem as Pandavas might not keep cool for long so asked Duryodhana to provide an alternate to release Pandavas from the slavery. Duryodhana discussed with his brothers and Shakuni and agreed to release them from the slavery provided they remain in exile for thirteen years with a condition that they will be incognito during the thirteenth year. Moreover, if their identity was revealed during the thirteenth year, they would have to go again in exile for the next thirteen years as he was sure that Pandavas will never be able to hide themselves.

History also blames Dhritrashtra for not stopping Duryodhana as he was the king and father of Duryodhana. History also did not forgive Bhishma and Dronacharya though both were great warriors but kept silence for the sin committed before them that too by their own grandsons and students.

History also did not forgive Yudhishthir not only for his weakness of gambling but also for his cowardice who himself remained silent on the insult of Draupadi and did not allow his brothers to take revenge.

Mahabharat war was now visible.

CHAPTER SIXTEEN

Krishna understood that the war was inevitable though many, even today, feel that war could have been avoided by Krishna. This was also expressed by Gandhari, mother of Kauravas after the war but Krishna knew that the war could be avoided but not the humiliation, insult, and sin committed by Kauravas with Draupadi and Pandavas. Probably insult done before family members could have been forgotten by Pandavas being their brothers but not the one done before others. Probably, Pandavas could forget their own insult but not of Draupadi.

The insult of Draupadi by Duryodhana and Dushashan was a heinous crime and stripping her was a sin against the culture, religion, society and humanity. Such a crime was not forgivable even by an ordinary person what to talk by the great warriors like Pandavas, and then by her father Drupad and his sons. Therefore, fight between Pandavas and Kauravas was inevitable in which Drupad and Karna could not be left out. Since others also jumped in the fight due to their insult in the past like Drupad and Dronacharya, Dhristdumn and Shikhandi, Shikhandini and Bhishma, Karna and Pandavas, Jaydrath and Pandavas, it converted into a fierce battle called Mahabharata war from a family dispute.

Some joined the war due to being close relatives of either Pandavas or Kauravas like Shalv, brother in law of Pandu who wanted his nephews Nakul and Sahdeva to become heir of Pandu, Shakuni who was against the marriage of his sister to a blind Dhritrashtra, Kumar Uttar who was brother in law of Arjun's son Abhimanyu, Kripacharya brother in law of Dronacharya, Satyaki and Kritvarma of Yadav dynasty and relatives of other princes and kings. Since all these were ruling almost entire territory of the country, family fight converted into a great war fought at Kurukshetra.

Here was the case of humiliation, insult, crime and sin. Since elders were silent spectators of such crimes, they also had to pay the price as it is the responsibility of the elders to intervene in case young do not follow the virtuous path. Thus, they were also responsible for the eruption of war.

Probably, Pandavas and Kauravas could have fought when Draupadi was being stripped and few would have died. But that was not feasible at that time as death also comes when God wants.

And death was to come during Mahabharat war for those who died in it.

Lord Krishna only knew what was going to happen as He was the creator, sustainer and destroyer.

CHAPTER SEVENTEEN

Krishna had warned Yudhishthir to remain vigilant from Duryodhana as had come to know about the incidence between Draupadi and Duryodhana. Yudhishthir was well aware about the attempt of eliminating Pandavas made by Duryodhana in *lakshagriha*. Still, Yudhishthir accepted the proposal of playing the dice.

Destiny prevails.

Krishna tried to avoid war between Pandavas and Kauravas on all occasions but such heinous crime against Pandavas and particularly Draupadi happened in his absence though he had warned Yudhishthir to be careful from Duryodhana before leaving Indraprastha but all went in vain.

Krishna knew very well that war was going to be fought immediately after completion of Pandavas' exile as he was a great visionary. Therefore, he suggested Pandavas to prepare for the battle with Kauravas and utilize period of their exile in obtaining weapons and making friends. He also told that they must keep patience for thirteen years as this situation had arisen due to their own fault of accepting the proposal of gambling. Also, they should not get depressed else they would not be able to achieve their goal. Specially, he asked Arjun to utilize each and every moment of his exile of thirteen years for preparation of the war as he knew that Arjun would play a vital role in Mahabharata war.

Pandavas decided to leave their mother Kunti, wife Draupadi and Arjun's wife Subhadra at safe places so that they can remain in exile concentrating in the preparation of war. They had no trust on Duryodhana now and Dhritrashtra was blind while Gandhari had tied her eyes so they left their mother with Vidur. Draupadi did not agree to live without them so they had no choice but to take her. Pandavas decided to leave Subhadra with her brother Krishna.

During exile when they visited Dwarka, Krishna again stressed for the utilization of the exile period for *tapasya* (penance, or practice for the desired purpose), getting divine weapons, and making relations with the kings. He also advised them to practice continuously with the weapons.

Pandavas acted upon the advice of Krishna and got weapons from saints and deities during their exile, particularly Bhima and Arjun.

Bhima married to Hidimba, a princess of asur dynasty and had a son named Ghatotkach from Hidimba who was very powerful.

Arjun worshipped Lord Shiva and obtained weapons. He also went to Amravati (Indralok) and got divine weapons from Kuber, Yam, Varun, and Indra. Indra advised him to learn dance from Chitrasen.

Sometimes, we feel that some of the events happening in our life have no relevance as we are unaware of the future. If something is coming on its own and even don't look relevant immediately but do not harm us, these should be welcomed. Arjun learnt dance which helped him during incognito period.

CHAPTER EIGHTEEN

Pandavas were living miserable life in the forest with Draupadi, serving to sages, sometimes living in their ashrams and practicing weapons. They had to go out for arranging the food.

One day, Pandavas went out to arrange food leaving Draupadi alone at the ashram and requested sage Trunabindu and Dhaumya to look after her.

Jaydrath who was married to Dushala, Duryodhana's sister, was passing through that area. Thus, he was a close relative of Pandavas also. He went to Pandavas' place and found Draupadi alone. Draupadi tried to welcome him as he was her relative too. But, finding her alone he abducted Draupadi and started taking her to his kingdom. She cried but saints could not stop him.

When Pandavas returned to their place and came to know about Jaydrath visiting their place and abduction of Draupadi, they chased him and brought Draupadi and Jaydrath back. Pandavas slammed him on the ground and kicked him. Thereafter, Bhima shaved his hair leaving five tufts and left him before saints and his soldiers. Thrusting him in a chariot in chains, Pandavas allowed him to go to his kingdom with his soldiers.

Jaydrath had misbehaved and insulted Draupadi, his own relative and sister in law.

And Pandavas were so furious that they decided to punish him immediately and not only punished but insulted him.

Remember, insulted person is more dangerous than a living or dead.

Reaching his kingdom, Jaydrath handed over the kingdom to his wife and went for tapasya (penance) to take revenge from Pandavas.

And Jaydrath waited for the opportunity of taking revenge from Pandavas that came in the form of Mahabharat war.

CHAPTER NINETEEN

Duryodhana might have thought that Pandavas would not get adequate food and will not be able to fight in long run. He was also sure that he would be able to find out them during thirteenth year of incognito.

Pandavas also understood that during exile period, it would be difficult to fulfil their food requirement and if they remained busy in making arrangements of food, they will be finished for fighting the battle. Krishna also knew it so he advised Yudhishthir to pray to Sun god for the help.

Yudhishthir prayed accordingly and Sun god gave him a magical vessel known as *akshay patra* and made him clear that it would provide as much food as required everyday but before it was cleaned. Once cleaned, it won't provide further meal during that particular day. Yudhishthir handed over the vessel to Draupadi telling her the condition. Draupadi always had meals in the last and cleaned it only after everybody had finished the meal including the guests if any. Soon this was known to all so also to Duryodhana. Duryodhana was upset as his plan appeared to have failed about Pandavas starving during the exile period.

Once, sage Durvasa came to Hastinapur with his disciples. An idea to harm Pandavas came in the mind of Duryodhana. He provided the best hospitality with all kinds of food to sage Durvasa and his disciples. He became very happy from his hospitality and asked Duryodhana to demand whatever he desired in blessing. Duryodhana requested him to provide Pandavas a chance of his service the next day. Sage Durvasa accepted his request.

Duryodhana continued the hospitality in the morning so that he reached to Pandavas in the afternoon when Draupadi might have finished her meal and cleaned *akshay patra* so that Pandavas would not be able to provide meal to sage Durvasa and his disciples. Everyone was aware that sage Durvasa was highly short tempered and in case of noncompliance of his directions, he would give curse whosoever he maybe. Duryodhana anticipated if Pandavas would not be able to provide meal to sage Durvasa and his disciples, he would certainly give curse to them.

Sage Durvasa reached to Pandavas place when Draupadi had finished the meal and cleaned up the vessel. Durvasa told Draupadi that he and his disciples would be their guests today and would take meals after taking bath and then they went to take bath in a river. Draupadi became afraid of sage Durvasa as she had nothing to serve them.

Finding no alternative she remembered Krishna.

Krishna came there and asked for meal from Draupadi stating that he was very hungry. She became annoyed and asked him from where she would provide meal to him and instead of solving her problem he was increasing it. Krishna laughed and asked her to bring *akshay patra*. He saw that one grain was stuck at its bottom. He took it out and ate. As he ate, everybody's hunger including of sage Durvasa and his disciples was over and they felt as they had already finished their meals. Sage Durvasa meditated and realized the reason so did not return to Pandavas.

Never waste even a single food grain as it can even satiate the hunger of God.

CHAPTER TWENTY

When twelve years of the exile period were completing, Pandavas decided to go to a small kingdom away from relatives and friends as advised by Krishna. They decided to go to Viratnagar, Matsa kingdom ruled by king Virat.

For Pandavas, it was difficult to hide their identity due to their personality so they decided to change their identity. Yudhishthir went to the king as a court adviser with a false name as Kankanbhat. Bhima went as a cook with a false name as Vallabh. Arjun in woman's dress went as a dance teacher with a false name as Brihannala. Nakul became a horse keeper and trainer with a false name as Granthic and Sahdeva a cowherd boy with a false name as Tantipal. Draupadi went as a maid to the queen with a false name as Sairandhari. Since, Arjun could have been identified because of his body structure, he changed his form as eunuch.

Duryodhana had anticipated Pandavas to go to Dwarka, Panchal or any other kingdom of their relatives or to their friends. He had already sent his spies to such places but was getting no news of them. Time was passing and Duryodhana was getting nervous. He could not understand how Pandavas were able to hide themselves particularly Arjun as he was very handsome and had marks of bow (Gandeev) on his shoulder. Since male members at that time wore no clothes on upper part of the body, he was easily identifiable.

Since Pandavas were passing the life of serving others, they could have felt humiliated many times, eager to take revenge from Kauravas.

One day Keechak, queen's brother and the commander in chief of the army of Viratnagar forcefully tried to make relation with Sairandhari (Draupadi). Draupadi somehow managed to get out of his clutches by telling him to meet on a particular day and time. She then told the incidence to Bhima and sent him in her place. Though Keechak was very powerful, Bhima killed him. Duryodhana became suspicious on killing of Keechak as no citizen of Viratnagar could harm him. He believed that Bhima might have killed him as he had higher muscle power than Keechak. He became suspicious that Pandavas might be hiding in Viratnagar.

Thirteen years were coming to the end and Duryodhana had no time to send spies and wait. So he attacked Viratnagar to enter into the city, on the pretext that their soldiers had stolen their cows though no such incidence had occurred. Kauravas arrested king Virat as he was no match to the army of Hastinapur. Then his son Kumar Uttar went to fight with Kauravas but ran away looking to the mighty army.

Draupadi was keeping record of each day of their exile period. She calculated thirteen years and told Pandavas about completion of the incognito period. She told Kumar Uttar to take Brihannala with him and go to the battlefield as she knows someone who can fight with Kauravas. Reluctantly, Kumar Uttar took Brihannala as his father had been arrested.

On the way, Arjun revealed his identity to Kumar Uttar and thereafter Arjun defeated Kauravas army.

Arjun also declared that Pandavas had already completed the period of their exile.

Knowing identity of Pandavas, Virat married his daughter Uttara to Abhimanyu, the son of Arjun and Subhadra.

CHAPTER TWENTY-ONE

Pandavas remained in exile for thirteen years including last one year in incognito as per the condition of Duryodhana for getting back their kingdom. But Duryodhana was upset as he had never thought that Pandavas would not be recognized during incognito period. Since he had multiple resources, he was sure that their spies would easily be able to search them.

And just after the exile, Pandavas showed their superiority in Matsa kingdom of Virat by way of Arjun defeating the army of Kauravas. Kauravas had thought that after thirteen years of exile, Pandavas will be very weak and no match to Kauravas. Actually, the planning of Duryodhana had failed. Due to failure of his planning, Duryodhana might have felt embarrassed before his brothers, and friends.

As handing over Indraprastha to Pandavas was not in the Kauravas' plan, they retracted and Duryodhana refused to hand over Indraprasth to Yudhishthir.

After other mediators failed to convince Duryodhana, Krishna offered himself to Pandavas to make a last attempt by going himself to Hastinapur and talking to Dhritrashtra. Pandavas agreed and sent Krishna formally to meet Dhritrashtra and Duryodhana.

Krishna went to Hastinapur as a messenger of peace. By now, Duryodhana was taking many decisions on behalf of Dhritrashtra in consultation with Shakuni, Karna, and

Dushashan.

As a messenger of peace, Krishna pleaded to Dhritrashtra to return Indraprastha to Pandavas as per the commitment. It is said that Dhritrashtra told Krishna that the decision is to be taken by Duryodhana as he had won the game and made the commitment. He did so due to fear or attachment to power or his son, cannot be said but it was not an act of a king.

Krishna tried to plead Dhritrashtra and Duryodhana to return Indraprastha to Pandavas but Duryodhana flatly refused and Dhritrashtra showed his helplessness.

Then, Krishna asked them to settle for five villages in favour of Pandavas but that too was declined by Duryodhana. Finally, Duryodhana told Krishna that he would not give land even equal to a point of a needle to Pandavas. Probably, Duryodhana still not forgotten his humiliation and insult, and wanted to eliminate Pandavas. Duryodhana declared that he would give nothing to Pandavas without war.

Duryodhana thought Krishna was on the side of Pandavas so ordered his soldiers to arrest Krishna.

To his surprise, the soldiers could not even dare to come near Krishna due to radiant energy emitting from his body. The emitted energy was so much that even those sitting in the court were unable to bear his effulgence.

Krishna laughed at Duryodhana and returned back from Hastinapur. He told the decision of Kauravas to Yudhishthir.

Mahabharat war was close by.

CHAPTER TWENTY-TWO

Kauravas and Pandavas were the relatives of Krishna. So Duryodhana and Arjun tried to garner his support. Krishna's army was very strong and powerful so both Pandavas and Kauravas wanted to get his support.

Duryodhana and Arjun both knew that Krishna would help them so they went to Dwarka as Krishna was the king of Dwarka.

Duryodhana reached the palace first and went in but Krishna was sleeping. He sat on his head side and waited Krishna to get up. After a while, Arjun reached there. Arjun always treated him as his elder and guru so sat down on his feet side. When Krishna awoke, he saw Arjun first and asked the purpose of his coming. Suddenly, Duryodhana spoke and told that he had come earlier and wanted to make a request first. Krishna said that he would like to fulfil demand of both but as he had seen Arjun first so let Arjun be given chance first. Krishna then told that he would keep his powerful army on one side and he alone without picking arms during the war would be on other side. Duryodhana became nervous as he wanted to choose for his army but Arjun was asked to make choice first.

Arjun chose Krishna and Duryodhana became happy to receive powerful army.

Thus Krishna's army went to Kauravas. Satyaki, a commander of Yadava's army disassociated from taking part from the Kauravas' side and joined army of Pandavas being a strong follower of Krishna.

CHAPTER TWENTY-THREE

Pandavas and Kauravas were to choose chiefs of their armies. Duryodhana knew that Bhishma was attached to the throne so he made him chief of his army. Bhishma agreed with the conditions that he would not harm to Pandavas and Karna will not be in the army till he was the chief. Duryodhana had no choice so agreed as he was aware that many kings may not support him if Bhishma was not made the chief.

Pandavas discussed the matter with Krishna. He suggested the name of Dhristdumn as chief of their army as Dhristdumn was the son of Drupad, and brother of Draupadi and Shikhandi who were eager to take revenge from Bhishma and Dronacharya.

Kurukshetra was chosen as the battlefield. Both the parties agreed to code of conduct prepared by Bhishma. Code of conduct included that the war would be stopped after sunset and both the sides would then be free to meet each other and then no one would harm others. It was also decided that unarmed soldier would not be attacked and fight would be on one to one basis between warriors and equal rank and status. The warrior if dislodged from the chariot will be allowed to take another one before restart of the fight. Yudhishthir and Duryodhana agreed to the code.

Krishna then offered himself as charioteer of Arjun. Arjun was happy as he knew the importance of a charioteer who could save the fighter from the direct attack. Krishna knew that Arjun was to play a major role in winning the battle of Mahabharat war but was also highly emotional. Hence, he would require guidance and lessons from him so he chose to become his charioteer.

CHAPTER TWENTY-FOUR

Kauravas and Pandavas garnered support from all the corners. Everyone took part except Balram, elder brother of Krishna. Rukmi who was brother of Krishna's wife Rukmini and Vidur.

On the first day of Mahabharat war, Duryodhana was satisfied with the strength of his side as it included Bhishma, Dronacharya, Karna, Kripacharya, Ashwatthama, Shalv, Vikarna, Bhurisrawa and Jaydrath. Pandavas army included Dhristdumn, Satyaki, Virat, Drupad, Dhristketu, Cekitana, Purujit, Kuntibhoj, Saibya, Yudhumanyu, Uttamauja, Abhimanyu.

To commence the battle, Bhishma from Kauravas side and by Arjun from Pandavas side blew their conches. Then Arjun requested Lord Krishna to place his chariot between both the armies so that he could have a look at those he is required to fight.

Lord Krishna then placed the chariot between both the armies. Arjun saw Bhishma, Dronacharya, his elders, teachers, maternal uncles, brothers, sons, grandsons, friends, father in laws and others assembled there to fight. Seeing them, Arjun told Lord Krishna that his mouth was drying up, limbs weakening, body trembling, skin burning and Gandeev slipping from his hands, his mind becoming unsteady, not desiring victory, even kingdom or joy of winning. He told that he did not see any good in slaying his own kinsmen even for the victory of kingdom of the three worlds. And Arjun kept his Gandeev aside.

Arjun was not at all ready to attack or counterattack respected grandfather Bhishma and Guru Dronacharya.

Lord Krishna told him about his emotional weakness overpowering his worth before the enemy. He told that everyone present there was existing at all the time and will exist in future also. Just as the body changes from childhood itself to youth and old age, soul also migrates from one body to another. Soul is always live and the body is not soul. Soul does not have grief or pleasure. It is the body sensing cold, heat, pleasure, and pain which are temporary in nature.

Soul is imperishable and indestructible and without soul, body is dead. No one can destruct soul. Soul neither slays anyone nor can slay anyone. Soul neither takes birth nor dies at any time as is immortal, everlasting, imperishable and timeless. Though soul is source of life, it never dies on destruction of body. No one can cause death to soul even if someone slays a person. Weapons cannot harm soul, fire cannot burn it, water cannot wet it and air cannot dry it up. Soul is invisible, inconceivable, and immutable. Therefore, one should not mourn for it.

Human beings know only the events between birth and death but not those before the birth or after the death.

If you do not fight as fighting the battle is your duty here, you will lose your reputation and incur a sinful action. Then, people will speak insulting words and humiliate you forever.

Lord Krishna told that you cannot renounce performing action as nothing can be achieved without performing action. And action has to be a virtuous action.

You should perform your action without desire of its result. Perform your virtuous action offering it to God as a sacrifice as various activities in the universe are driven through sacrifice or offering to others.

Lord Krishna said, if you have desires of performing action, you will be attached to its result. And, the lust or desire arising out of extravagance is the greatest enemy to oneself being insatiable and extremely sinful as it covers the wisdom even of a knowledgeable person engaged in controlling senses and mind.

Lord Krishna told Arjun that death is certain for living ones. Even those assembled here do not know about what happens before the birth and after the death. I am aware of my births and also yours but not you.

The one who renounces desire of the result of action is always a renunciate and is free from the dualities. One having renounced virtuous action is not knowledgeable as the knowledgeable performs virtuous action.

Arjun, momentary pleasures arising from the sense gratification are indeed the source of misery, having a beginning but short end. A self-controlled person able to control physical, mental and emotional urges produced from the material desires and attachments remains happy. One who experiences internal happiness, able to see self within as well, having reached to self-realization stage, working for the welfare of all living bodies, free from lust, fear and anger, having controlled mind, desires and senses, performing meditation certainly understands the Ultimate truth.

Everything is manifested, created, sustained and destroyed in the universe by two energies, inner energy and external energy. There is nothing superior to inner energy and everything is connected through it like pearls by a thread. This energy is contained in origin of all living bodies, providing wisdom and prowess. Even satgun (verity), rajogun (extravagance) and tamogun (vileness) temperaments are from this energy but they are not in this energy.

Complete universe gets deluded from the external energy, but no one knows inner energy, superior to external energy, supreme and indestructible.

The one who is able to remember God at the time of death achieves God's gesture as one remembers that time what has been absorbed by him through continued contemplation. Therefore, remember God all the time, and fight dedicating your mind and knowledge unto Him.

Lord Krishna showed Arjun the Ultimate form which had innumerable heads, faces, mouths, eyes, arms in all the directions with innumerable rare weapons, thousands of suns simultaneously blazing around Him, complete universe situated in Him at a small place along with all species of the living entities, sages, deities, having no beginning, middle or ending. Then Arjun saw one of fiery mouth in which family members, relatives, friends, kings and soldiers standing before him in the battlefield were entering and perishing. Thereafter, he started trembling looking to death God in Him and asked Him to reveal His identity. Lord Krishna told that those whom he is looking perishing are actually going to die soon whether he fights or doesn't. Therefore, you be the medium and conquer the enemy including Dronacharya, Bhishma, Jaydrath, Karna as their death has already been designed by Him.

Ultimately, Arjun picks up his weapons and get ready to fight.

CHAPTER TWENTY-FIVE

With Krishna's discourse and motivation, Arjun picked up his weapons and started fight. Since it was the first day, the strategy of the opposition was not clear to both the parties but Bhishma was a great warrior and strategist so was successful in his plan. First day is considered in favour of Kauravas as Bhishma killed many soldiers of Pandavas' army. Also, both the sons of king Virat were killed on the first day. Therefore, Pandavas changed their strategy and decided that Arjun will directly fight with Bhishma and prevent him fighting with others.

The result of the strategy was visible the next day and Pandavas' army suffered much less loss compared to the first day. Still Bhishma was killing many soldiers of Pandavas' army as Arjun was not able to stop Bhishma completely.

On day three also, many soldiers of Pandavas' army were killed. Though Pandavas were also killing soldiers of Kauravas' army but it was the fourth day when Bhima killed eight brothers of Duryodhana and thus personal loss to Kauravas and Pandavas started.

And thus battle continued. On eighth day, Arjun's son Iravan (son from Ulupi, naga princess) was killed. In the evening, Bhishma vowed that he would force Krishna to take over weapon knowing fully that Krishna had promised not to take part in the battle and pick up the weapons.

Bhishma started fierce battle next day and Krishna knew why Bhishma was furious as he wanted him to retreat on his promise and pick up the weapon. Bhishma was a great warrior and everyone including Lord Krishna knew that Bhishma, once vowed, shall fulfil his vow at any cost. Bhishma was known for his promise. He had promised to his father never to marry and had sacrificed throne of Hastinapur for his step brother in the honour of his father. And thereafter also, he continued to obey to his step mother considering as his own mother. He was fighting from the side of Kauravas only due to his promise as he had vowed to guard the king of Hastinapur irrespective of the person who was occupying it.

When Krishna saw Bhishma getting furious, he thought for the welfare of others. For fulfilling the promise of Bhishma and protecting many others, he broke his promise and took wheel of the chariot in his hand.

This is the major difference between a human being and God. A human being tries to fulfil own goal at the cost of others while God thinks for the welfare of others even at his cost. Lord Krishna was not being aimed by Bhishma and had nothing to worry but took wheel for others. And it was known to Bhishma also that Lord Krishna had taken up wheel only to fulfil his vow and therefore as he took wheel in his hand, he stopped the fight as his mission was fulfilled. Lord Krishna also did not throw wheel on Bhishma as he also knew that neither he needed to throw wheel on Bhishma nor Bhishma wanted to fight with him. Therefore, Krishna is God who broke his promise for Bhishma while Bhishma remained a human being in spite of the fact that he forced Lord Krishna to pick up the wheel breaking up his promise.

Thereafter, Pandavas got worried as they knew that it was impossible to win against Bhishma as he was blessed to choose the time of his death. So they asked Krishna for the plan. Krishna knew how Bhishma would die but he didn't want to reveal it so he advised Pandavas to go to Bhishma and ask him. Krishna knew that Shikhandi would be the cause of his death and Bhishma would not fight Shikhandi as he still considered him a girl.

Bhishma did not disappoint Pandavas and told them that he would not fight directly with Shikhandini, now Shikhandi. So Pandavas made a plan. They knew that Shikhandi's arrows could not affect his body so next day Arjun kept Shikhandi in front of him and started fight with Bhishma. When Bhishma saw Shikhandi, he stopped fight while Arjun had left his arrows which pierced Bhishma. Bhishma immediately understood that arrows were not of Shikhandini but of Arjun. He fell down on the ground with pierced arrows in his body but did not die as he had a boon of dying according to his will.

Battle was called off immediately on that day and both sides rushed their medical help to Bhishma but he refused for help and told others that he would not die immediately and therefore they should not worry for him.

CHAPTER TWENTY-SIX

On eleventh day, Dronacharya was made commander of Kauravas' army. Karna also joined as Bhishma was no more the commander.

Thus, war continued while Bhishma was lying in the battlefield. In the evening, Dronacharya and Karna along with Duryodhana made a plan to capture Yudhishthir as capturing candidate for the throne would lead to their win and then they could force Pandavas to agree to their conditions. But they knew that their plan would not be successful till Arjun is away from the battlefield so they made a plan to keep him away.

Kauravas contacted king Bhagdutt and forced him to attack Arjun and take him away from Kurukshetra. According to the plan, Bhagdutt attacked Arjun and took him away from Kurukshetra. Dronacharya then decided to adopt *Chakravyooh* formation as he was aware that nobody except he himself and Ashwatthama from Kauravas and Arjun and Krishna from Pandavas' side knew how to break *Chakravyooh*.

On thirteenth day, Dronacharya put his army in *Chakravyooh* formation. As no one from Pandavas' army knew how to enter, they were helpless and could not find any clue to enter inside and fight with those who were attacking them. Dronacharya and Duryodhana were sure of the success from their plan of capturing Yudhishthir and winning the war that day. But Abhimanyu, son of Arjun and

Subhadra told to Yudhishthir that he knew how to enter the *Chakravyooh* but was unaware of the exit. Since Kauravas' army was killing Pandavas' army, they had no clue what to do so decided that main warriors of Pandavas' army would enter *Chakravyooh* along with Abhimanyu and protect him at all costs.

Abhimanyu entered in the *Chakravyooh* but others could not as they did not have any clue of entering in it as in no time Kauravas' army sealed the entry. Abhimanyu was alone inside *Chakravyooh* and started fighting with Kauravas' army. He fought almost full day.

Dronacharya and Duryodhana failed to reach Yudhishthir as everyone was engaged in the fight with Abhimanyu. In the last, Abhimanyu was surrounded inside the *Chakravyooh* by all main warriors of Kauravas' army but as he had no knowledge to exit.

Main warriors including Jaydrath and Karna attacked Abhimanyu and Jaydrath killed him when he was unarmed and without chariot in presence of all other warriors including Karna.

Abhimanyu was killed when he was alone and unarmed which was against code of conduct.

On that day, code of conduct was shattered.

When Arjun came to know, he vowed killing Jaydrath before the sunset of the next day else of dying by setting fire on himself.

Ethics were not expected from Duryodhana but certainly from Dronacharya. Dronacharya with whom Arjun was reluctant to fight, Dronacharya for whom Arjun had fought with Drupad, Dronacharya whom Arjun respected most.

Dronacharya and Duryodhana did not follow ethics and sent Arjun away from the battle. They did not follow ethics and witnessed killing of unarmed Abhimanyu.

When ethics are not followed, codes, manuals and standard operating procedures (SOPs) do not work. Bhishma had ethics and therefore, during first ten days, code of conduct was followed and he knew that Karna will also not follow ethics in the battle so he prevented him fighting along with him.

Surprisingly, Dronacharya also did not follow. Probably, he had no sympathy to Pandavas now as Drupad was with them.

CHAPTER TWENTY-SEVEN

Next day Dronacharya and Kauravas changed the strategy and decided to use Arjun's vow for their success by protecting Jaydrath till sunset. Accordingly, they surrounded Jaydrath and protected him from all around with their army.

Again it was against the code of conduct as each warrior was supposed to fight on one to one basis but now the ground rules were breaking. Arjun was stopped by the army of Kauravas to reach Jaydrath and Jaydrath did not come out from the bunker. Kauravas were desperate for the sunset.

In the afternoon, suddenly it became dark as sun has set.

When it became dark, Arjun asked his soldiers to set fire but Krishna asked Arjun to sit on fire with his bow and arrows. Nobody could understand how suddenly sun had set. It is said that Krishna put his *Sudarshan Chakra* in between Sun and Earth and it became dark. Probably, there was solar eclipse on that day. Whatsoever was the reason, it became dark and arrangements of fire were commenced for Arjun.

Duryodhana and Karna with all Kauravas' army became overjoyed and wanted to enjoy the moment so gathered at the place where Arjun was setting fire on himself. They also asked Jaydrath to witness the death of Arjun.

Jaydrath came there and saw Arjun getting ready to enter into the fire. He started laughing and commented that it was not the day of his death but of Arjun.

Pandavas were shocked and were unable to utter even a word. Lord Krishna was as calm as ever. Suddenly sun started shining as the eclipse was over. It is also said that Lord Krishna removed his *Sudarshan Chakra*. Everyone was taken by surprise. Lord Krishna said to Arjun to look up. When Arjun saw sun shining and Jaydrath laughing before him, he shot an arrow towards Jaydrath killing him then and there.

Kauravas were taken aback. By the time they were in senses, Jaydrath was dead. Duryodhana seeing his brother in law killed, asked his army to take up the battle. He was fumed from the death of Jaydrath and that day battle continued even after the sunset by Kauravas. Thus, ground rules and code of conduct were torn off to pieces.

Duryodhana was so furious that he asked Karna to use his divine weapon against Arjun that day itself. Just then Ghatotkach, son of Bhima and Hidimba, started fight killing Kauravas' army as he would finish entire Kauravas' army that day itself. Duryodhana then asked Karna to use divine weapon against Ghatotkach and he did so.

Ghatotkach was killed by Karna that night but had lost divine weapon kept reserved for killing Arjun.

CHAPTER TWENTY-EIGHT

By fifteenth day, sons of Arjun, Bhima and Duryodhana all were killed.

Dronacharya killed Drupad.

Dronacharya loved his son Ashwatthama and was always worried of his wellbeing. He was a close friend of Duryodhana. Though Arjun took revenge from Jaydrath for his son's death, he knew that Dronacharya deliberately created *Chakravyooh* on the day when he was not in Kurukshetra and was also responsible for manipulating his departure from the battlefield thus responsible for Abhimanyu's death. So he told Krishna that he considered Dronacharya and Karna also responsible for the death of Abhimanyu.

Arjun was aware now that Kauravas had started breaking ground rules and code of conduct. Now, Pandavas were also ready for the same.

Pandavas adopted a trick for weakening Dronacharya as he had adopted a trick to send Arjun away from the battle and form *Chakravyooh* in his absence. Pandavas asked Bhima to kill the elephant named Ashwatthama and spread the news of the death of Abhimanyu before Dronacharya.

Bhima killed the elephant and started shouting that Ashwatthama had been killed. When Dronacharya heard it from Bhima, he did not believe so confirmed from Yudhishthir. As per the plan, Yudhishthir replied "Yes, but the elephant". He said "yes" in normal voice "but the elephant" very softly like murmuring. Same time all the warriors of Pandavas' army blew their conches so Dronacharya could not hear "but the elephant". He was so shocked and grieved that he kept his weapons aside for a while and Dhristdumn killed him immediately to take revenge of the insult of his father, Drupad.

CHAPTER TWENTY-NINE

On sixteenth day, Karna was made supreme commander of Kauravas' army. Kunti met him in the previous night of his taking over the command and revealed that he was his son. As such, he should not fight from Kauravas' side and harm his own brothers. Karna said that he always treated his foster parents as his real parents. And she was known the mother of five Pandavas in public so he assured her that her five sons would remain alive as he would not kill any of the Pandavas except Arjun. He also told her that he would not leave his friend Duryodhana's side. Next day he fought bravely and wounded Yudhishthir, Bhima, Nakul and Sahdeva but did not kill them keeping his promise.

On seventeenth day, fierce battle started between Arjun and Karna. Lord Krishna had earlier told Arjun that Karna was a great warrior, a great archer and in no way less than him and thus he should fight with his full strength. The fight was between Karna and Arjun, two great warriors, two great archers, and two real brothers. Everyone from both the sides was stunned to see the strength of two great warriors. In the last, Karna left the arrow and Arjun's chariot was pushed a little back, the chariot which was being driven by Lord Krishna himself so immediately Lord Krishna admitted his power and strength. In response, Arjun left the divine arrow which led to his chariot rooted inside the ground. Karna got down to take out the chariot by lifting its wheel.

Arjun killed him remembering killing of Abhimanyu, against the code of conduct.

And Bhima killed Dushashan that day.

One should select his friends very carefully as good friends take one to heights but even a bad friend sinks one even if in possession of great skills, strength and power. Whenever Karna was alone, he never misbehaved or insulted anyone but when he was with his friend Duryodhana, he had no control on his mind.

CHAPTER THIRTY

On eighteenth day, Shalv took over as the commander of Kauravas' army. Even though maternal uncle of Nakul and Sahdeva, he was fighting from Kauravas' side thus against his own nephews. Shalv was no match to Bhishma, Dronacharya or Karna. Kauravas also realized that the war may be over any time.

Sahdeva killed Shakuni.

Yudhishthir killed Shalv.

Bhima killed all remaining brothers of Duryodhana.

All the warriors from Kauravas' side were slain. Duryodhana was not even aware about the warriors who were still alive from his side so he fled and took refuge in a lake. Bhima chased Duryodhana and challenged him.

Bhima and Duryodhana then fought fiercely. Suddenly, Bhima remembered his vow of breaking thigh of Duryodhana and hit mace on Duryodhana's thigh remembering the insult of Draupadi as he had asked Dushashan to bring Draupadi and made her sit on his thigh. Though striking below waist by mace was against the rules. Duryodhana was wounded and Bhima left him bleeding.

Mahabharat war was now over.

But killing and revenge did not stop with the end of Mahabharat war.

Ashwatthama and Kritvarma met to Duryodhana and promised him to take revenge from Pandavas though Mahabharat war was over. They attacked Pandavas' palace in the night, again flouting all the rules and killed many soldiers including Dhristdumn, Shikhandi and five children of Draupadi.

Dhristdumn, son of Drupad died.

Shikhandi died.

Children of Draupadi died.

And Duryodhana died.

Insult done to Amba, Dronacharya, Drupad, Duryodhana, Karna, Pandavas, Kauravas, Jaydrath and Draupadi resulted into many deaths including of near and dear ones. Shikhandini incarnation of Amba, Dronacharya, Drupad, Dhristdumn, Duryodhana, Karna, Jaydrath, all Kauravas, and all sons of Pandavas died in Mahabharat war.

But everything was still not over.

CHAPTER THIRTY-ONE

Ashwatthama then tried to kill Uttara, pregnant wife of Abhimanyu to finish family and heirs of Pandavas though killing a lady or unborn child was considered against the ethics and morality and was a sin. Lord Krishna saved her and Abhimanyu's unborn son also. Uttara's son was named Parikshit.

Ashwatthama was a great warrior, very intelligent and knowledgeable but in the company of Duryodhana, he could not control his mind. He committed such a ghastly sin for which he is still remembered and blamed. Uncontrolled mind always covers wisdom and knowledge.

And at the end of eighteenth day, survivors were five Pandavas, Krishna, Satyaki, Ashwatthama, Kripacharya, Yuyutsu, Kritvarma and Vrishketu (son of Karna whom Pandavas gave patronage).

CHAPTER THIRTY-TWO

After the end of Mahabharat war, Lord Krishna met Kunti and Gandhari. Gandhari was the mother of Kauravas and had lost her sons and only son in law, Jaydrath in Mahabharat war. Though she respected Lord Krishna but was of the view that he could have avoided Mahabharat war and then her sons and son in law would have been alive. So she was in great anger and grief due to their death. When Krishna came to meet her and paid respect, she cursed him for the destruction of his family and Yadav race fighting among themselves like soldiers and family members of Hastinapur had died. She also cursed that as her sons and relatives had died fighting among themselves, his family and relatives would also have same fate.

Lord Krishna accepted the curse. That was the greatness of Lord Krishna that even without of his fault, he accepted the curse of a lady. Then he told Gandhari about his efforts to avoid Mahabharat war and tried to persuade Duryodhana and Dhritrashtra to offer five villages to Pandavas but they did not agree. He also narrated the incidences when Kauravas tried to kill Pandavas in *lakshagriha* and other time still he tried to mediate between them. He told that he extended help both to Kauravas and Pandavas in the form they demanded.

Gandhari had cursed Lord Krishna in anger but then she realized that it was not Krishna but actions of Duryodhana and her other sons responsible for Mahabharat war so she apologized to Krishna but Lord Krishna told her not to regret as the curse had to come as that was to happen.

Destiny prevails.

CHAPTER THIRTY-THREE

Yudhishthir became the king of Hastinapur.

Pandavas gave full respect Dhritrashtra and Gandhari as their parents and took care of them after Mahabharat war.

Mahabharat war took lives of many soldiers from all over the country. Loss was so huge that even today it is considered most devastating war. Description of Mahabharat war is given in Mahabharat epic.

CHAPTER THIRTY-FOUR

Yadav soldiers who survived from Mahabharat war became proud and considered themselves powerful. As other powerful kings had died, they started disrespecting sages, elders and saints in the pride of their power.

Power corrupts powerful.

Krishna had a son named Samba from the queen Jambvati. One day, Samba dressed himself like a pregnant woman and started playing with his friends. Great sages were going to Krishna including Durvasa, Vashishth, Narad and Vishwamitra where Samba met them. He joking asked them to predict the gender of the unborn child.

He might have thought of humiliating sages on their reply.

The sages realized everything but kept mum. When Samba insisted to tell to whom she would give birth, they became angry and cursed him that he would give birth to an iron piece that shall destroy entire Yadavas' race.

Samba and other boys got afraid when they saw that the cloth piece tied by Samba had converted into iron piece. Samba did not go to Krishna but went to Ugrasen and informed him about it. He advised him to grind the iron piece and throw it into sea. He did accordingly. Lord Krishna came to know about it but remained silent as he knew that his time to go from the earth had come.

Suddenly bad incidents started. People started misbehaving and insulting elders. Satyaki insulted

Kritvarma criticizing him for taking side of *adharma*, and getting involved in killing innocent children when they were asleep. Kritvarma also argued and then started fighting themselves. In the fight, Satyaki killed Kritvarma. When other Yadavas saw Satyaki killing Kritvarma, they killed Satyaki. Soon, all the inebriated Yadavas started fighting themselves and died except Vabhru, Daruka, Balram and Krishna.

Balram, Vabhru and Krishna also left this world next.

It is said that after mere thirty-six years of Mahabharat war, no Yadav was alive so also the Pandavas as they embarrassed death by climbing on Himalaya.

Humiliation and insult always lead to destruction.

Always remember: "No Humiliation and insult please."

Please Do not Humiliate and Insult Anyone

Printed by Libri Plureos GmbH in Hamburg, Germany